Manu c

CW00449149

Manchester EveningNews M EN media

THE VOICE OF MANCHESTER

Manchester EveningNews city

WE HATE IT WHEN OUR EX-LODGERS BECOME SUCCESSFUL

Cheers Ta Publications

www.cheersta.co.uk

To absent friends,
particularly Diké Omeje and Hovis Presley.

First published in 2008
by Cheers Ta Publications
Cheers Ta House
10 Merston Drive Manchester M20 5WT

All layout and design by solutions2design

A CIP record for this book is available from the British Library
ISBN 978-0-9536392-3-6

acknowledgements

I would like to say a big thank you to Mike Garry, fellow Manchester
poet and all round top bloke, for having the energy and enthusiasm to
make this publication possible. To Ant Ball at Summerhouse in
Manchester for all his work that went into the design of the book.
(I took the photos, though, and I'm dead pleased with myself.)
To Andy and Mick also at Summerhouse - cheers for the endless tea
and banter. Also, a big thumbs up to my poetry chums dotted around
the country, but particulary (and in alphabetical order) Rob Cochrane,
Julian Daniel, Tony Kinsella, James Quinn and Max Seymour. A "big up"
(or something similar) to Darren Conway, everyone who's helped me at
Apples and Snakes, Commonword and Write Out Loud. Thanks also to
everyone who's "employed" me down the years, at poetry events,
comedy clubs, schools, libraries, prisons and so forth. It's been loads
of fun, well, most of the time anyway. A big thank you to Stephen
Hewitt for years of help with the flow of bizarre ideas and to Tony
Ashton and Bren Lynch for acres of laughs and allowing me to doss
down in my home city all those times. Thanks to Claire, Kieran and
Eleanor for managing to put up with me all this time and a big thumbs
up to everyone who knows me.

Apologies to my dad Brian, who brought me up better than to use
some of the swear words that are asterisked out in certain poems
(but I'm afraid no other words would suffice).

Erm... Hope you enjoy the book. The limericks in here were originally
published by The Bad Press as a boxed set called "Making Prawn
Sandwiches For Roy Keane." They are the pick of that collection.
Imagine what some of the others were like...

Love, peace and crisps,

Marvin

December 2008

PS...www.marvincheeseman.com (thanks to the brilliant Martyn
Whittaker plc, cheers for back cover pic too Martyn, chip cone on way)
myspace/marvin cheeseman (Thanks to that Tom bloke)

contents

AQUARIUS

A voice from your dim and distant past will re-surface on your voicemail this week. Or answer machine thing. Whatever you do, don't respond. Ostensibly, they are merely attempting to renew your acquaintance.

In reality, they're on a week long training course next month at an agricultural college only four miles from you, and need a place to crash. Do you really want them necking your Cabernet Sauvignon and being lavish with the heating and lighting like there's no tomorrow, or carbon footprint implication?

Didn't think so...

And if you're wondering what happened to that family bag of Twiglets on Friday, you'll find them under the front passenger seat of your silver Audi A3.

PISCES

It might be a good idea to have several dozen sheets of your favourite lavatory paper about your person on Tuesday. Don't ask, just trust me on this one.

Tuesday could also turn out to be the right day for revealing your true feelings about someone you've recently grown fond of.

Or is it?

Their response might not be quite what you anticipated. The truth can often be unpalatable, maybe better just to keep your trap shut instead.

On the other hand, faint heart never won fair lady, nothing ventured nothing gained, it's
better to shoot and miss than not shoot at all, you've got to be in it to win it.

But having said that...

ARIES

It doesn't have to be springtime to have a spring clean, but seeing as it's your birthday on Tuesday and therefore very much springtime, there's no excuse for not getting your finger out and tackling that mound of crap you refer to as "belongings". The 536 CDs crammed under your bed would be a useful place to start.

Don't kid yourself you'll sell some on ebay, get some cardboard boxes and take a load round to Oxfam. One note of caution: don't discard anything too hastily, especially "Static And Silence" by The Sundays. (How did you end up owning that?) Conversely, anything bearing the words "Phil" and "Collins" next to each other, can be jettisoned with total confidence.

One other thing, don't forget to take a sample with you to Dr Radwinski's on Wednesday. Make sure it's properly sealed this time. We don't want a repeat of last month, do we?

TAURUS

Just because you've always done something in a particular way you shouldn't make the mistake of thinking that there isn't another way of doing it. However, that doesn't necessarily mean that you should try doing things in a different way just for the sake of it. It could well turn out that the particular way you've always done something is the right way to do it after all. We all know how unlikely that is, though, don't we?

The moon moves into Libra on Saturday, so you'll need all your diplomacy skills to settle a dispute concerning ownership of a half-eaten Twix.

You will also get a very unexpected, enviable, once in a lifetime opportunity to slap the ex-footballer and TV, "personality" Gary Lineker. If you can't bring yourself to slap him, then at least throw a drink over the ****.

GEMINI

A mega week - in fact a truly unforgettable and unprecedented week, in terms of relationships. Or a relationship. You need to bite the bullet, lay all your cards on the table, grab the bull by the horns and start checking your emails on a much more regular basis. It's now or never, make or break, shit or bust.

Just one other thing, don't make the mistake of thinking you've seen every single episode of Columbo.

There's one on ITV this Sunday, where the murderer (or murderess in this instance) - a Mrs Williams - takes Columbo up in a light plane and puts the wind up him a bit. It's one of the earlier and therefore superior ones too –1971 if I'm not mistaken.

Enjoy...

CANCER

Is it a sprain or is it a break? Putting weight on it only intensifies the pain. You're heading for casualty or accident and emergency, or whatever they call it these days. This isn't any metaphorical nonsense either.

You really will be sorting out a mess with the NHS, to describe it in something of a freestyle manner.

Take a thick book, a big flask, maybe a ham salad sandwich or at least a packet of Mini Cheddars. You'll be there for the duration.

Saturday is their busiest night (apart from Friday, though Sundays can be surprisingly hectic as well) and there's no jumping the queue: you're not a celebrity, you're definitely not royalty, you're just a forgettable, nondescript, insignificant member of the public.

Other than that, not a bad week.

LEO

Venus is travelling through your romance zone right now, so perhaps it's time for some new underwear. In fact it's time for some new underwear anyway, regardless of where Venus is. You should have got round to it when the sales were on like you meant to.

You've been very upbeat and invigorated just recently. Try to temper your ebullience. Several of your colleagues rightly suspect that you've been on the old Columbian Marching Powder again and will be trying to tap you for some.

On Thursday, there's bad news in the form of a bank statement. However, this will only prove to be a temporary setback. As per usual, you land on your feet with a completely unexpected and thoroughly undeserved stroke of luck.

You stuffy bastard. You make me sick…
you really do.

VIRGO

Don't bother recording Coronation Street on Wednesday when you're at judo. You'll only be coming home to random excerpts from Chelsea v Olympiacos. You've absolutely no interest in football, not only that but the game will be a frustratingly tepid 1-1 draw.

This situation highlights your distinct lack of organisational skills, and you need more than a copy of TV Quick to prick that particular boil.

The recurring nightmare you've had recently where you're a dinner lady constantly trying to prevent Jamie Oliver from spitting on a pile of sausages will soon stop. Don't be unduly concerned, it's definitely not your fault and it's a surprisingly common complaint amongst men your age.

LIBRA

It's high time for a long, hard and honest look in that full-length mirror. It's even higher time for some personal re-invention and revitalisation.

A thorough top-to-toe makeover is called for, but where the hell do you start? Liposuction would be top of my list, then some Anne Robinson style reconstructive surgery, some cosmetic dentistry wouldn't go amiss either, not forgetting a new hairstyle, a complete new wardrobe of tasteful clothes (that'll be a first) and a few dozen elocution lessons.

You won't recognise yourself and even better than that, neither will anyone else.

Who says you can't polish a turd?

SCORPIO

A neighbour of yours is going on holiday soon and will foolishly ask you to water their plants, look after the dog, or feed the fish; but not all three, though possibly two from these three. You, me and your Uncle Bernard (from bitter experience in his case) know only too well the full extent of your ineptitude in such matters.

You'll have to invent some sort of half-arsed excuse (thankfully, this is one area in which you excel).

It's far better to sidestep this situation now than have them return from Magaluf to something dead, almost dead, or shrivelled up to buggery. Let them down gently by offering to "keep an eye on the house." This will make you sound considerate, but is essentially an empty gesture, involving no effort whatsoever on your part.

One other thing, Flora Pro-Activ may indeed lower cholesterol, but that doesn't mean you should be getting through a tub a day.

SAGITTARIUS

That recent underlying feeling of discomfort you've been experiencing finally subsides on Wednesday when the moon leaves Uranus.

Try not to kick off at the Spar shop some time round the middle of this week when once again they'll be out of crumpets. Once more they'll be suggesting fruit teacakes as an alternative.

Just count to ten and "suck it up" as our American friends are fond of saying. "Suck it up" essentially means that the situation is beyond one's control, nothing can be done to retrieve the situation, it's best just to accept what's happened and keep one's composure.

And another thing… next time crumpets are available, why not buy an extra pack or two and freeze them?

Other than that, it's a fairly quiet sort of week.

CAPRICORN

You are self confidence personified this week.
You're at the peak of your powers, the top of your
game. You exude charisma from every orifice.
The sun has got his hat on whenever you're around.

Or at least that's what you think…

Most of your colleagues find you to be a
constant and detestable source of irritation, whilst
the remainder can barely tolerate you.
It's high time for a holiday, so get on the net, get on
Ceefax, just get something booked as soon as, and
give everyone an effing break…

If you're not away by Wednesday, be wary of a
clumsy, bearded Sagittarian making a chicken
noodle Cup-a-Soup.

A BURLY YOUNG FARMER FROM BRISTOL

A burly young farmer from Bristol
Won a beautiful vase made of crystal
But what gets on his tits
Is he blew it to bits
Whilst arsing about with a pistol.

A CELIBATE MAN FROM CARACAS

A celibate man from Caracas
Found an unsightly rash on his knackers
He knows he'll get cured
Of that he's assured
But how it got there is driving him crackers.

A DISGRACED EX-ART TEACHER FROM BRIGHTON

A disgraced ex-art teacher from Brighton
Could not get to sleep with the light on
He couldn't eat cheese
Identify trees
Or watch TV when there was shite on.

A FARMER WHO CAME FROM SEATTLE

A farmer who came from Seattle
Had a terribly large herd of cattle
For miles they would roam
But he knew they'd got home
When his ornaments started to rattle.

A YOUNG CHAP FROM NEAR ABERGELE

A young chap from near Abergele
Did impressions of folk off the telly
He was first to admit
They were mostly all shit
Though he did quite a good Matthew Kelly.

A TRIBUTE TO ROY KEANE

He played in midfield not up front
His tackles were frequently blunt
He took a dim view
Of the prawn sandwich crew
And he called Mick McCarthy a ****

A TRIBUTE TO WILLIAM SHATNER

Captain Kirk was considered a looker
But when he became T J Hooker
I think Mr Spock
Would have got quite a shock
At this podgy wig-wearing old ****ker.

A TRIBUTE TO NORMAN WHITESIDE

United fans loved Norman Whiteside
When he scored they could look on the bright side
But he piled on some weight
Drinking beer by the crate
And his kit looked a bit on the tight side.

A TRIBUTE TO REGINALD BOSANQUET

Reggie was reading the news
Apparently worse for the booze
The viewers all heard
The words that were slurred
But could not see the piss on his shoes.

THERE WAS A YOUNG MAN FROM PRESTATYN

There was a young man from Prestatyn
Who slept in pyjamas of satin
Pyjamas as clean
As you've ever seen
Apart from the night they were shat in.

THERE WAS A YOUNG LAD FROM DEVIZES

There was a young lad from Devizes
Wrote poems to try and win prizes
But the judges weren't smitten
With the stuff that he'd written
A lot of it didn't even rhyme.

A TRIBUTE TO RICHARD WHITELEY

Richard Whiteley was not very sprightly
The clothes that he wore were unsightly
Yet despite his apparel
He was always with Carol
And for that, I envied him slightly.

PRIMARK - THE RUMBLE IN THE JUMBLE

Queues as far as the eye can see
Clothes so cheap they're almost free
High Street Heaven for the skint and thrifty
Five pairs of knickers for one pound fifty

Cut-price clobber rail after rail
A fifty-two week long January sale
Shameless shoppers soon succumb
To the large-scale jumble sale rugby scrum

Denims and tempers are equally frayed
Impeccable manners rarely displayed
A jostle here, an elbow there
In love, war and the process of frenzied sartorial
consumer transactions, all is fair

Manic men with psychotic spouses
Rabidly rummage through mounds of trousers
Marks and Spencer hit for six
By the very antithesis of Harvey Nicks

Garment garlands garnish the floor
I trip on pyjamas for a girl aged four
Grab what you can, then run out fast
How much longer will this madness last?

It's a bargain bonanza that can't be resisted
You'd think branded clothing had never existed
Shirt, shoes, kecks and a coat
I still had change from a five pound note.

LET THERE BE LIGHT

Be it council flat, castle or thatched-roof cottage
Let there be light at a responsible wattage

Let there be light...
But mind how you go
Ensure the dimmer switch is set nice and low

Let there be light...
Banish the gloom
Just don't burn a bulb in an empty room

Let there be light...
Treasure each ray
Harness the solar stuff during the day

Let there be light...
Let's get it right
The future's bright

But hey...

Not that bleedin' bright.

TAT OR TREASURE

(written for Dickinson's Real Deal ITV antiques programme.)

Clear out your clutter, don't twiddle your thumbs
Old telescopes make astronomical sums

The earthenware vase that was pulled from a skip
Would be worth seven grand if it didn't have that chip

A Chantilly teapot in the Japanese style
Serves as a doorstop for a bloke in Carlisle

There's lots to think about and lots at stake
Is that Claude Lorrain mid-seventeenth century painting
"Pastoral Landscape With Ruins" real or fake?

Clear out your clutter from your car boot trips
Is it dearer than diamonds or cheaper than chips?

You've got to find out what the experts reveal
At David Dickinson's Real Deal.

LET ME DIE A COWARD'S DEATH

(after Roger McGough)

Let me die a coward's death
Not a brave and bullet through the chest death
Just a comfy snug tucked up in bed death

When I'm 73, and constantly knackered
May I just slip away in a slumber sublime
Having savoured a Horlicks for the very last time

Or when I'm 87, and doubly incontinent
May I give my hot water bottle one final fill
And never re-awake to feel its wretched chill

Or when I'm 103, and having lost each and every
one of my marbles
May I kick the bucket gently and not know a thing
Having set the clock to never hear it ring

Let me die a coward's death
Not a messy, mangled by machine death
Just a muffled cough then shuffled off death.

ON THE SUPERIOR NATURE OF FOSSIL FUELS

There's no fuel
Like an old fuel.

ADVOCAAT

Advocaat…
My first sip aged seven
Sent my taste buds straight to
Paradise
It was so nice.

Advocaat…
A kind of alcoholic custard
That really cuts the mustard.

Advocaat…
Not a drink you'd think of first
In a desert dying of thirst.

Advocaat…
Bought from Spar, supped by Ma
But not with pate de foie gras.

Advocaat…
I love it, I rate it
I completely advocate

Advocaat.

WITH APOLOGIES TO NINA SIMONE

My baby don't care for clothes
My baby don't care for shows
So when I turned up in my Armani suit
With front row tickets for "Phantom Of The Opera"
I must have looked like a right tw*t.

I JUST HAD THE STRANGEST DREAM

I once had a dream about Clement Freud
Hard to believe but it's true
On the night of the second of April
In the year 2002

It's hard to remember much detail
Though he'd asked me to make him some tea
He wanted Earl Grey or Darjeeling
But all I had in was PG

His bald head was shining quite brightly
(Clement wasn't wearing a hat)
I once had a dream about Clement Freud
You can't get more Freudian than that.

CRAIG DAVID GETS FOOD POISONING

(with thanks and apologies to Cath Sim)

Did a roast chicken on Sunday
Loads of it left over on Monday
Had some with a salad on Tuesday
Fridge was on the blink on Wednesday
Chanced it in a curry on Thursday
I was throwing up on Friday

And Saturday

And Sunday…

…not to mention shitting through
the eye of a needle.

DOROTHY PARKER TYPE FOOTBALL POEM

Footballers don't make passes
To team-mates who wear glasses…
…Unless it's Edgar Davids.

THE QUEEN'S GOLDEN JUBILEE MANCHESTER HAIKU

under the bunting
assorted Mancunians
slowly get bladdered.

HEAVEN KNOWS I'M MIDDLE CLASS NOW

I was happy in the gloom of a Netto store,
but heaven knows I'm middle class now.

I was looking for some wine, a decent
Sauvignon Blanc, and heaven knows Netto didn't
have any.

In my life, why should I waste valuable time, in
supermarkets that only stock one type of hummous?

I was looking for a school to send my daughter to
that wasn't over-run by Chavs.

I was looking for a school and then I found a school,
but heaven knows I had to up sticks and move to a
different catchment area.

In my life, why should I give valuable time, to people
who wear nothing other than gymnasium clothing?

I used to think the rich should subsidise the less
well off, but heaven knows I'm all in favour of the
abolition of inheritance tax now.

I used to get The Mirror but now it's The Daily Mail,
'cause heaven knows I'm a shallow, self-obsessed,
uncaring, narrow-minded, thoroughly obnoxious,
totally despicable, Nazi bastard now.

SOME PEOPLE JUST CAN'T GET OVER THINGS

On the wall in a frame is a goldfish
The kids couldn't quite say goodbye
Some people just can't get over things
Some folk just can't let it lie.

Down below, alas, stuffed and mounted
Rex is on permanent show
Some people just can't get over things
Some folk just can't let it go.

To the left is an urn on a plant stand
Filled with ash, Auntie Flo long since gone
Some people just can't get over things
Some folk just cannot move on.

To the right in a tank of formaldehyde
Uncle Stan's wearing only a beard
Some people just can't get over things
Some folk are just ****ing weird.

IF OUR LOVE WAS...

If our love was a car...
it would be a brown, 1986 mini metro
and the driver's door would be beige.

If our love was a television...
the corners of the screen would be rounded and it
would only receive Channel 5.

If our love was a school report...
it would contain more Es than a Pot Noodle

If our love was a professional footballer...
it would be sat on the sub's bench wearing a
Luton Town shirt.

If our love was a supermarket...
it would be Netto.

If our love was an item of jewellery...
it would only be available in Argos.

If our love was a celebrity...
it would be Mark Lamarr.

If our love was a random antique article picked out
by a contestant on *Bargain Hunt*...
it would make a loss, at auction, of £115.

And if our love was a butterfly...
it would be a Heath Fritillary:
drab, seldom seen and always on the brink of extinction.